SCIENCE INVESTIGATORS

Investigating FORCES and MOTION Through Modeling

Kristin Thiel

Cavendish Square
New York

Published in 2020 by Cavendish Square Publishing, LLC
243 5th Avenue, Suite 136, New York, NY 10016

First Edition

Website: cavendishsq.com

Library of Congress Cataloging-in-Publication Data

Names: Thiel, Kristin, 1977- author.
Title: Investigating forces and motion through modeling / Kristin Thiel.
Description: First edition. | New York : Cavendish Square, 2020. | Series: Science investigators | Audience: Grades 5 to 8. | Includes bibliographical references and index.
Identifiers: LCCN 2019014520 (print) | LCCN 2019018859 (ebook) | ISBN 9781502652454 (ebook) | ISBN 9781502652447 (library bound) | ISBN 9781502652430 (pbk.)
Subjects: LCSH: Force and energy--Models--Juvenile literature. | Motion--Models--Juvenile literature. | Physics--Experiments--Juvenile literature.
Classification: LCC QC73.4 (ebook) | LCC QC73.4 .T435 2020 (print) | DDC 531/.6078--dc23
LC record available at https://lccn.loc.gov/2019014520

Editor: Caitlyn Miller
Copy Editor: Nathan Heidelberger
Associate Art Director: Alan Sliwinski
Designer: Ginny Kemmerer
Production Coordinator: Karol Szymczuk
Photo Research: J8 Media

The photographs in this book are used by permission and through the courtesy of: Cover Svetik/Getty Images; p. 4 Fuse/Getty Images; p. 9 Stock Montage/Getty Images; p. 10 Spencer Grant/Getty Images; p. 13 Snapgalleria/Shutterstock.com; p. 15 Eyepark/iStockphoto.com; p. 16 John Slater/Getty Images; p. 17 Science Source; p. 20 Tom Merton/Getty Images; p. 22 Elisabeth Schmitt/Getty Images; p. 23 Adam Nieman/Science Source; p. 25 2800x1866 Cultura/Newscom; p. 28 Jupiterimages/Getty Images; p. 30 NASA/Science Photo Library/Getty Images; p. 32 Francisco Soberanis/Shutterstock.com; p. 34 Carrin Campanelli Photography; p. 35 Yodchompoo/Shutterstock.com; p. 37 Nasky/Shutterstock.com; p. 39 iStockphoto.com/eskaylim.

Printed in the United States of America

Contents

Forces and motion affect all areas of our lives, including sports!

CHAPTER 1

Key Concepts

Force and motion are a part of every moment of your life. Even right now, as you sit in a chair reading this book, forces are happening. Your body is applying downward force to the chair. The chair is applying upward force to your body. You are also in motion, even though you have not taken a step. You are sitting on Earth's surface. Because Earth is constantly moving, you are moving too. The reason you don't notice is that our planet spins on its axis at basically the same speed all the time. We only notice motion when speed changes.

THE POWER OF FORCES AND MOTION

Sometimes forces and motion are hidden, but they are always important. Consider bridges. Gravity is constantly pulling down on bridges. Bridges do not touch the ground in many places, so they cannot easily push up against gravity. Yet most bridges stay standing. They do so even with the extra weight of people and vehicles crossing them. Bridges do this by balancing two kinds of forces: compression (squeezing inward) and tension (stretching outward). Some parts of the bridge compress. Some experience tension.

Now imagine a football game. Force is obvious because players tackle each other. Motion is obvious too. A running back heading for the end zone with the football tucked under his arm does not want to stop running. He does not want to stop being in motion. He won't stop—unless a force (like a member of the other team's defense or gravity itself) gets in his way.

NEWTON'S THREE LAWS OF MOTION

These common examples of force and motion are related to basic principles of physics. Three of these principles are called Newton's laws of motion. Sir Isaac Newton was born in England in the 1600s. He was a scientist interested in objects, energy, and how they interact. In other words, he studied physics.

Newton figured out three important rules, or laws, about how the world works.

Newton's first law of motion says that an object that is not moving will remain still forever—until something moves it. A football sitting on the field will never start moving on its own. A football player has to pick it up, or the wind has to blow against it. In the same way, an object that is moving will stay moving in that same direction forever—or until something else pushes or pulls it or gets in its way. Football players running for the end zone demonstrate that an object in motion will stay in motion, unless they are forced to stop by the other team's defense.

Newton's second law says how far and fast an object moves depends on its mass (which is a measurement of how much matter an object contains) and how hard it is pushed or pulled. How well a football kicker positions himself and how long his foot is in contact with the ball make a difference when it comes to how far that football can travel. The second law also provides the math that proves that different objects will react in different ways to the same amount of force. Imagine throwing a football. Now imagine balancing a watermelon in your hand and throwing it with the same amount of force. The football will move faster and farther than the watermelon.

Newton's third law says that for every action, there is an equal and opposite reaction. A football player who runs into another player had better be prepared to bounce backward himself. Even if you go lie down in bed and fall asleep, your body and your bed will continue to exert force against each other.

FORCE AND MOTION HELP US SOAR

Newton built the foundation. Now, scientists are expanding on his understanding of force and motion in all sorts of ways. Astronauts landed on the moon and NASA has explored Mars because its scientists understood the forces of gravity and rocket fuel and the motion of planets.

Today, coaches help athletes perform better, and sports engineers and designers create more useful shoes, equipment, and facilities. These experts all think about biomechanics, which studies the body's movement. That's just some of what is possible because we understand force and motion. There is a lot to explore!

The Models of Isaac Newton

Isaac Newton developed ideas about motion in the 1600s that we still use.

Modeling is an important part of researching and experimenting. Scientists use models to explain things. Models help them describe and demonstrate complex ideas. Models can be made from objects, be simulated on computers, or take the form of charts, graphs, and mathematical equations.

Isaac Newton modeled his three laws of motion in a smart way. He kept everything simple. He did not think of an object in motion or affected by force as having a particular shape or size. He did not think about where the object was or what other objects may be near it. He just thought of that object as a math problem. By doing this, he was not distracted by questions such as "What if the object were big?" or "What if the object were sticky?" This allowed him to understand the physics that affect all objects, no matter their size (or their stickiness). That's why his laws describe the primary characteristics that all forces and motions share.

The opposite poles of magnets attract. The north pole of one magnet is attracted to the south pole of another magnet.

CHAPTER 2

Modeling Magnetic Force

Magnetic force is the invisible power of attraction or repulsion between two objects. It makes objects come together or refuse to ever connect. Even thousands of years ago, people understood some of the practical uses of magnets. For example, many of the earliest explorers used magnets to make compasses to help guide their way.

UNDERSTANDING MAGNETISM

Even if you have been playing (and experimenting!) with magnets for years, you may not know the terms for what you have witnessed. Here are some facts:

The ends of magnets are called poles. One pole is north, and one is south. Magnets will only stick together by their opposite poles: one magnet's north pole connects to the other's south pole. When two poles repel each other, you cannot force those two magnets together. That is because you are trying—and failing—to put both north poles together or both south poles together.

The north pole of a magnet always points toward Earth's geographic North Pole, which is actually a magnetic south pole. That is because Earth contains magnetic materials. Early explorers used the science of magnetic force to navigate long before GPS was invented.

If you cut a rectangular bar magnet in half, you get two complete magnets. Each one has its own north and south poles. If you run a magnet over magnetic material, such as an iron nail, you can magnetize that item. In other words, you turn that nail into a magnet.

A magnet creates an invisible magnetic field around itself. You have probably noticed that you do not have to touch a paper clip with a magnet to get the paper clip to stick to the magnet. You just have to get the two items close to each other. Then, the paper clip "jumps" or "flies" to the magnet. Once the paper clip gets within the magnetic field, it is pulled to the magnet.

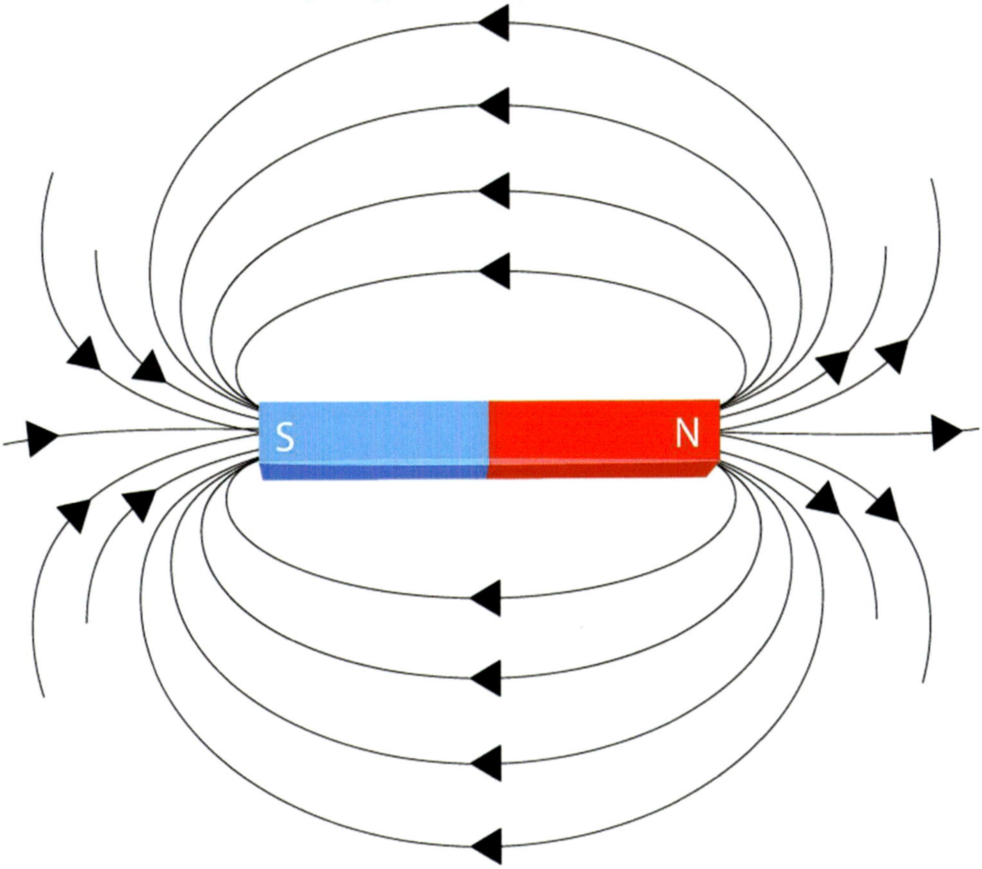

This diagram shows the magnetic field surrounding a bar magnet.

Magnetic fields can go through some objects. That is how a magnet can hold a piece of paper to a refrigerator. The magnet is not touching the refrigerator, but its field goes through the paper to touch the refrigerator. You can make a bigger magnetic field by putting two magnets together. Their combined magnetic field almost doubles the field of each magnet by itself.

MAKE YOUR OWN MODEL: THE "MAGIC" OF MAGNETS

Magnetic force is so interesting that it may seem magical. Even great philosophers and scholars have been amazed by its powers. However, magnetism can be explained by science. Magnetic force is real, and anyone can experiment with it. It is also replicable. Unlike a magic trick, a magnet "trick" can be performed over and over and will not fail. Magnetic force obeys the laws of physics, including Newton's laws of motion. You can make your own model of magnets in action.

Materials

ruler

blank piece of paper the same length as your ruler

tape (any kind)

pencil

plastic toy car

other small objects about the same size as that car (for example, an eraser, an empty matchbox, a different plastic toy car)

small bar magnets (they should all be the same; they should be no longer or wider than the car)

Directions

1. Tape your piece of paper to a flat surface, like a table.
2. Place your ruler along the long side of the paper. Make it even with the paper. Line up the ruler's 0 mark with one end of the paper. Line up the last number on its other end with the paper's other side.

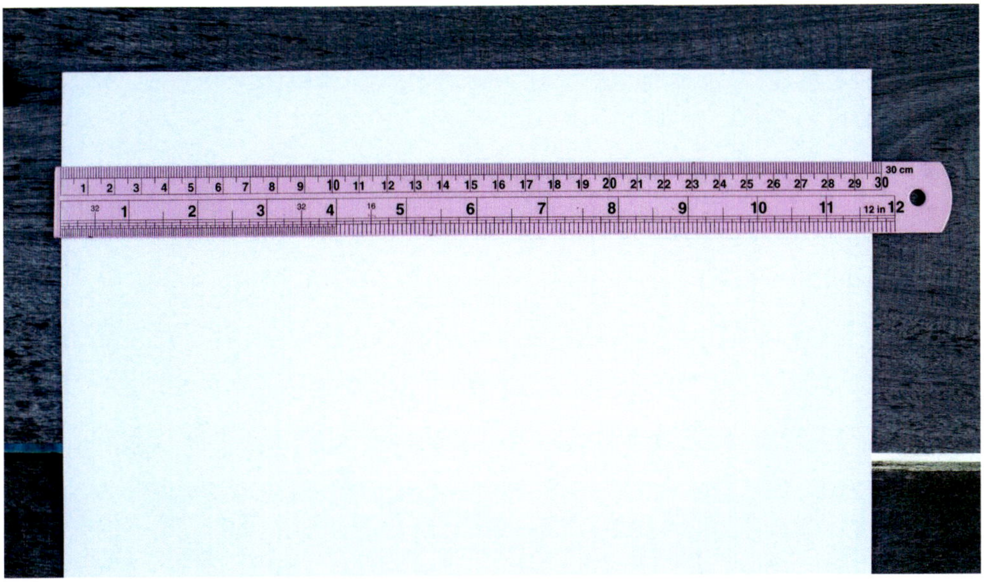

To get accurate results, make sure you line up your ruler and paper carefully.

3. Tape one magnet to the top of your plastic car.
4. Set the car just off the paper, so it looks like it is about to drive across the paper, next to the long edge of the ruler. The front edge of the magnet should be even with the edge of the paper and the mark on the ruler.

In this model, you'll need to make sure your toy car can roll easily before adding magnets to the setup.

5. Give the car a test run by tapping it forward gently with your finger. Does it easily drive onto the paper? If the edge of the paper catches its wheels, you may need to tape down that one edge of the paper. When scientists conduct experiments and use models, they often end up making adjustments. It is smart to take time to make sure your setup is working.

Now, try to move the car by magnetic force:

1. Take one of your other magnets in your hand. Which end should be aimed toward the car in order to attract the car's magnet? If the magnets' poles are not marked, you will need to test each one to see which end is north and which is south.

2. Hypothesize: How close does your magnet need to get to the car's magnet to move the car?

3. Hold the magnet facing the correct way in your hand. Place it opposite the car, at the other end of the paper and even with the mark on the ruler. Slowly move the magnet forward. When the car starts to move forward, stop moving your hand. Write down how far your magnet traveled beside the ruler.

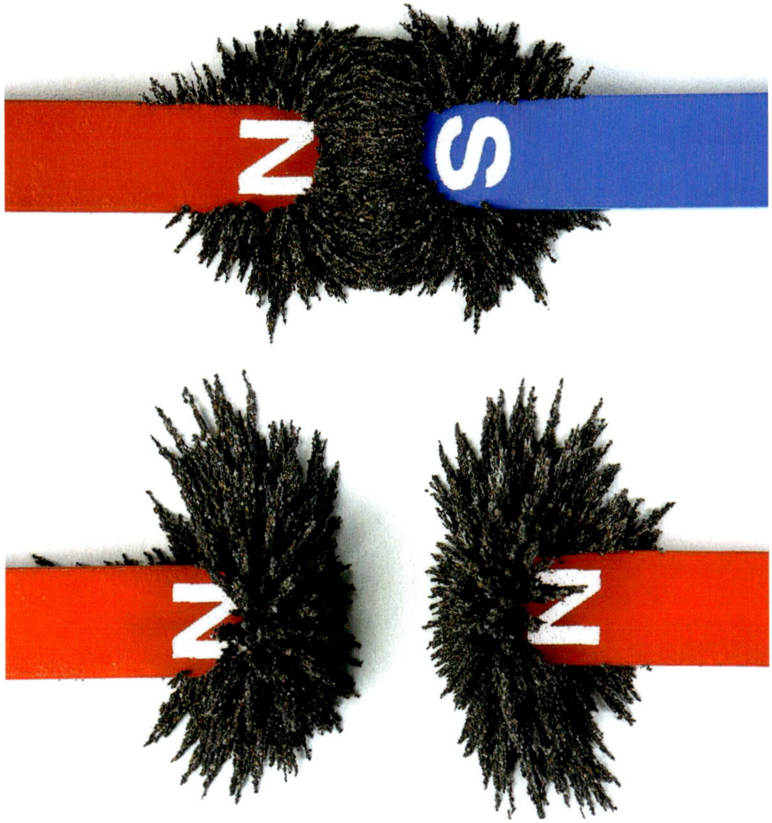

Remember that opposite poles attract (*above*), but two of the same poles will repel each other (*below*).

4. Put the car back where it started, and add a second magnet to the one in your hand, north pole to south pole. Hypothesize: How close does this new supermagnet need to get to the car's magnet to move the car? Repeat the experiment.

5. Again return the car to the beginning. Add a third magnet to the double-magnet in your hand. Repeat the experiment.

6. Each time, write down how many magnets you used, your hypothesis, and how close you had to get the magnets to each other to make the car move.

7. Add a magnet to the car and learn how that changes things.

8. Tape the car's magnet to one of the other car-size objects you brought. Again, start with one magnet in your hand. (Did you make sure you are pointing the right end at the object's magnet?) Hypothesize: How close does your magnet need to get to this object's magnet to move it? Slowly move your magnet toward the object until the object moves. Build up your magnet and keep repeating the experiment.

9. Now think about what you've seen. Predict how your results would change with items that are bigger or smaller. How would your results change with bigger or smaller magnets? What about if you used more magnets?

Test Yourself

1. How did you hold your magnet so it would attract the object's magnet?
2. Why did different objects move at different points?
3. Did adding magnets to your hand increase the strength?
4. How do magnets obey Newton's laws of motion?

Answers:

1. If the north pole of the object's magnet was aimed forward, the south pole of your magnet had to be aimed toward it. If the magnet's south pole was forward on the object, your north pole had to be. Remember: opposites attract.
2. Weight and friction (when one object rubs against another) can affect a magnet's ability to attract.
3. Yes. The strength of the magnetic field will nearly double if two magnets of the same shape and strength are joined.
4. Magnetic force can cause an object to change its state of motion (Newton's first and second laws), and it is an example of action and reaction (Newton's third law).

Understanding motion is as easy and fun as jumping!

CHAPTER 3

Jumping to Model Motion

To understand motion, it helps to understand a few terms. These words relate to speed, change in speed, and how much matter an object contains. All are very important to motion.

SPEED, VELOCITY, AND ACCELERATION

Speed is how fast something moves. For example, your bike's speed may be 8 miles per hour (13 kilometers per hour). Velocity is speed plus direction. Your bike's velocity may be 8 miles per hour (13 kmh) going north.

You can experiment with acceleration, deceleration, and velocity while enjoying a bike ride.

Acceleration is a change in velocity. If you want to bike faster than 8 miles per hour (13 kmh), you must pedal harder. Your bike might accelerate to 12 miles per hour (19 kmh) in the direction you are going. When you see a stop sign, you use your brakes. Your bike decelerates to zero miles per hour. You have stopped moving forward, so braking causes a change in velocity.

MASS

Mass affects acceleration. The more mass an object has, the more it resists changes to its motion, including changes to its velocity. Mass refers to the amount of matter in an object.

Mass multiplied by velocity equals momentum. Momentum indicates how difficult it would be to stop a moving object. When a quarterback throws someone a football, that football has momentum because it has mass and velocity, but the mass is relatively small. The player can catch that football and stop its motion. However, it is not as easy to stop a defensive player on the football field. This is because that player has a higher mass than that football.

This model shows the masses of the sun and other objects in space. The sun has the largest mass compared to Earth. Pluto has the smallest.

Many people confuse mass and weight or think they mean the same thing. However, weight is different from mass. Weight is a force. It is part of the attraction we all feel to Earth. Gravity affects weight, so weight changes depending on where an object is. For example, the moon's gravity is one-sixth as strong as Earth's gravity. Objects on the moon weigh one-sixth as much as they do on Earth. Remember that an object's mass doesn't change based on where it is. It is the same on Earth and the moon. Gravity is also connected to mass. A planet with more mass will have a stronger gravitational pull.

INERTIA: AVOIDING CHANGE

Inertia is related to mass. Newton's first law of motion explains inertia. It says an object at rest will stay at rest, and an object that is moving will keep moving, unless something changes that state of inertia. Inertia is resistance to change in motion. The more mass an object has, the more it will be able to resist changing motion. Inertial mass measures how difficult it is to move or stop an object.

Once acceleration and mass get involved, Newton's second law of motion comes into play. Multiplying acceleration and mass equals force. Force can overcome inertia and stop an object

You can see Newton's third law yourself with a skateboard, a ball, and help from a friend.

from moving; it can change the object's direction, speed, or both; or it can start the object moving.

Newton's third law of motion explains what happens to the object causing the force. If that object applies force to overcome another object's inertia, an equal and opposite reaction will happen for the object applying the force. This happens without fail, even if we cannot notice the reaction. If one object has a lot more mass than the other object, we do not perceive the reaction. For example, let's say you stand on the sidewalk and throw a ball to your friend to the east of you. You are anchored to the huge mass that is Earth. The ball is the only thing that seems to move. If you do the same action while you are standing on a skateboard, you will noticeably move backward as the ball you threw forward also moves. If two objects have similar masses, their opposite and equal forces will cancel each other out. That is why a book can sit still on a table. The book's push downward and the table's push upward are the same.

EVEN ASTRONAUTS FALL DOWN

We have all seen clips of astronauts leaping on the moon and somersaulting through the air in their spaceships. However, astronauts are human. Sometimes they soar, and sometimes they fall—just like the rest of us.

Search online for a video of the Lunar Olympics. In 1972, astronaut Charlie Duke and his mission commander, John Young, did some high jumps on the moon in celebration of the Olympic Games happening that year. These two astronauts had a lot of fun, until Duke fell down and thought he might have split his spacesuit. If you split your pants open in class, that may be embarrassing. If an astronaut does that in space, it can be deadly. Luckily, Duke's suit hadn't actually split.

One of the reasons astronauts may stumble in space is that gravity and weight are different there, but mass is the same. Astronauts on the moon are trying to move in familiar ways but in very different conditions than they are used to.

MAKE YOUR OWN MODEL: THE PHYSICS OF JUMPING

Charlie Duke's story is a great example of motion on the moon—both the ups and the downs. For your demonstration of vertical movement, you are going to focus on the ups—sometimes the way-ups!

Materials

several long pieces of paper or a roll of paper

measuring stick

tape (any kind)

pencil

Directions

1. Standing still, reach up as high as you can and touch the wall. Ask an adult to help you tape a piece of paper on the wall so that its bottom edge is as high

In this model, you'll be jumping indoors while imagining what it would be like to jump in space.

as you can reach. Then, holding a pencil, jump two or three times. Each time you jump, mark how high you can reach.

2. Take the paper off the wall and measure the distance from the edge of the paper—where you can reach when you are just standing—to your highest jumping mark. That is the height you can jump.

3. Now, working on a long piece of paper, mark approximately how high you might jump in different places around the solar system:

    Earth: your jumping height

    moon: 10 feet (3 meters)

    Venus: 1.5 feet (0.5 meter); this might be close to how high you can jump on Earth.

    Mars: 3 feet (1 meter)

    Jupiter: You hardly get off the ground!

    Titan (Saturn's largest moon): 13 feet (4 meters)

    Pluto: 26 feet (8 meters) You may need to abandon the paper and measure out into the hall and into the next room.

Even in low gravity, like on the moon, forces and motion affect us!

Test Yourself

1. Why could you jump a lot higher on Pluto than on Earth?
2. Why could you hardly jump at all on Jupiter?
3. Why don't astronauts float away when they jump on the moon?
4. What is the unit of measurement of force? (Clue: Sometimes, units of measurement are named after a person.)

Answers:

1. Pluto's gravity is only 6 percent as strong as Earth's.
2. Jupiter's mass is three hundred times Earth's mass. That means its gravitational pull is a lot stronger than Earth's.
3. Many people think the answer lies with their heavy spacesuits. That is incorrect. Spacesuits weigh 280 pounds (127 kilograms) on Earth ... but they weigh next to nothing within the moon's weak gravitational pull. Astronauts are not being held down by that weight. Instead, the pull of the moon's gravity, even though it is much less than Earth's gravity, brings them back to the lunar surface. If an astronaut got out of the range of an object's gravitational force, that astronaut would keep moving in the direction he or she was going, according to Newton's first law of motion.
4. The measurement is newtons (N), after Sir Isaac Newton, the physicist who explained gravity and the laws of motion.

The laws of physics explain why seat belts keep us safe.

CHAPTER 4

Modeling Force and Motion Together

Wearing a seat belt when you ride in a car is not only a good idea because of safety laws—it is also a good idea because of the laws of physics. Everything we know about force and motion supports the idea that wearing a seat belt will help protect you in an accident. It may even save your life.

In this chapter, you are going to make a model that shows why seat belts are so important. Things are going to get messy, so make sure an adult has helped you find a good place to work on your model.

MAKE YOUR OWN MODEL: THE IMPORTANCE OF WEARING A SEAT BELT

Materials

uncooked egg in the shell (you may want to have two or three eggs on hand)

small cart on wheels that can hold the egg (you can use a toy truck or make your own by attaching four wheels to a small container)

board to be used as a ramp for the egg cart

Your cart can be made from anything. It just needs wheels and to be big enough to hold an egg.

objects to support the ramp and to block the ramp at its base (such as several books)

newspapers or towels

Directions

1. Set up your ramp. Angle the board by lifting one end with something like a short stack of books. Spread newspapers or towels out around the lower end of the ramp, its base. Set a book or two on top of the newspapers or towels at the base of the ramp.

Set your ramp up at an angle with an obstacle at the base. Make sure the ramp is strong enough to hold your cart.

2. Get your egg ready. You may want to draw a funny face on it, or you can leave it plain. Set it in its cart. Make sure it is secure enough in its cart that it will not fall out as it rides down the ramp. Also make sure it is loose enough in the cart that it can fly out once it hits the obstacle.
3. Hold the egg in its cart at the top of the ramp. When you are ready, let the two go down the ramp together.

The experiment is successful when the cart carrying the egg hits the obstacle at the ramp's base and the cart stops moving while the egg keeps moving. It flies through the air and cracks on the newspapers or towels.

You may need to do a little experimenting with the angle of the ramp and the height of the obstacle at its base. You may also need to adjust the cart you use for the egg. That is what scientists do too—they are always doing test runs. Sometimes you first have to run experiments on your experiment to make sure its parts work.

How Does This Relate to Force and Motion?

Let's break down what happened with this breakable egg. The cart and the egg each have mass. That mass will not change. Newton's first law of motion says the cart and the egg will stay sitting at the top of the ramp forever. However, the force of you pushing the cart disrupts that permanent state of rest. The force of gravity also changes that rest into motion.

Now, you are demonstrating Newton's second law of motion. You could use math to determine how powerfully you need to push the egg cart (force). To do this, you would need to know the force of gravity, the egg cart's mass, and how fast and far you

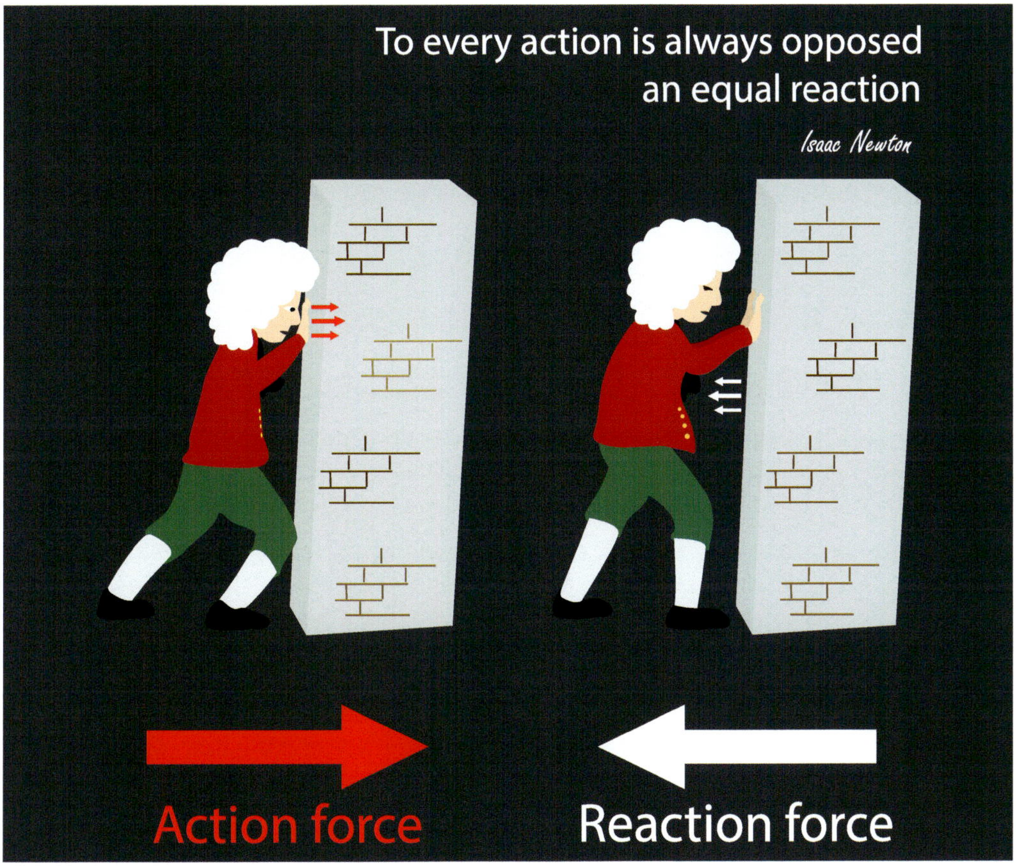

Isaac Newton's third law says that when you push against something, it pushes back on you with equal force.

want it to travel. For this model, you use previous experience with ramps and toy cars to estimate how much force is needed.

The cart and its egg passenger begin to move downward. They have motion and momentum. They travel at a speed in one direction, so they also have velocity. This is another example of Newton's first law—an object in motion stays in motion unless interrupted.

As the egg and the cart travel down the ramp, gravity pulls them, and the egg and the cart accelerate. Now, there is a change in their velocity. Next, the cart carrying the egg hits the obstacle at the end of the ramp. The cart bounces backward before stopping. That is an opposite and equal reaction to the action of striking the obstacle. This is an example of Newton's third law of motion.

Until this point, the egg appeared to be a part of the cart. Just as we move along with Earth, a car, or a bike, the egg was moving along with the cart. However, now we notice that the egg was not attached to the cart. It was not wearing a seat belt. When the cart strikes the obstacle, the cart's motion is interrupted—its inertia is disrupted. However, the force of the obstacle does not change the egg's motion.

The egg follows Newton's first law. It keeps moving. In this case, that means the egg flies out of the cart. At this point, the cart is also again experiencing Newton's first law—it is at rest against the obstacle and will remain that way until you move it.

Gravitational force acts on the moving egg and pulls it downward. In a dramatic display of Newton's third law, the egg cracks on the newspapers or towels. An eggshell is actually pretty strong if a force hits it evenly on its ends. It has a natural arch, just like many sturdy bridges do. A grown bird can sit

In this messy model, a broken egg is the goal!

on one little egg without breaking it. However, a tiny chick can also peck its way out of an egg. Similarly, the force of the ground pushing up against the egg is greater than the egg's force. The egg breaks.

Test Yourself

1. There are three laws of motion. Does an object always move in order through those laws? Give an example from this chapter's model.
2. Could you conduct this experiment on a flat surface, not a ramp?
3. If the egg were strapped to the cart, what would happen to the egg when the cart hits the obstacle?
4. If you did this experiment on the moon, what are some things that would be the same and different?

Answers:

1. An object demonstrates each law of motion many different times and in many different orders. For example, the egg and cart were at rest (Newton's first law). Then they experienced force to accelerate from rest to motion (Newton's second law). Once the cart hit the wall and stopped, it was back to Newton's first law: it stayed still.
2. Yes, but without gravity's extra help along the downhill ramp, you would need to use more force on the cart to get it to hit the obstacle hard.
3. The egg would stay in the cart. Because it would be attached to the cart, it would act as part of the cart. It would be stopped when the cart was stopped.
4. Everything would have the same mass. The moon's gravitational force would have less of an effect because it's one-sixth as strong as the gravitational force on Earth. You would move backward when you pushed the cart with its egg forward.

Glossary

acceleration A change in velocity.

attraction A force drawing two things together and keeping them from separating.

compression A force that presses or squeezes.

force An interaction between two objects that pushes or pulls and disrupts inertia.

friction Force that resists motion between two objects.

hypothesize To make a logical guess about what will happen.

inertia Resistance to change in motion or rest.

magnetic field The space around a magnet in which its magnetic force can be felt.

magnetize To make something that wasn't a magnet into a magnet through the power of magnetic force.

mass How much matter an object has.

model A tool used by scientists to understand or explain ideas.

motion Change in place; movement.

Newton's first law of motion An object that is not moving will not start moving by itself. An object that is moving will keep moving in the same direction unless something forces it to change.

Newton's second law of motion Force affects motion—an object will move farther and accelerate faster if it is pushed harder. Mass is important too. An object with more mass requires more force to accelerate.

Newton's third law of motion For every action, there is an equal and opposite reaction. If an object is pushed, an equal force will push back.

physics A field of science that studies matter, energy, and how matter and energy affect each other.

repulsion When equal forces push each other back.

velocity Speed in a particular direction.

Further Information

BOOKS

Gonick, Larry, and Art Huffman. *The Cartoon Guide to Physics*. New York, NY: CollinsReference, 2005.

Hollihan, Kerrie Logan. *Isaac Newton and Physics for Kids: His Life and Ideas with 21 Activities*. Chicago, IL: Chicago Review Press, 2009.

Sohn, Emily, Charles Barnett III, and Steve Erwin. *A Crash Course in Forces and Motion with Max Axiom, Super Scientist*. North Mankato, MN: Capstone Press, 2016.

WEBSITES

High Jump

https://cosmos-book.github.io/high-jump/index.html

Two astronomers, Stuart Lowe and Chris North, made an informative—and fun—interactive page about jumping in space.

Scholastic Study Jams! Force & Motion

http://studyjams.scholastic.com/studyjams/jams/science/forces-and-motion/force-and-motion.htm

Scholastic offers several interactive web pages on force and motion. From this page, you can "see all related jams" or type keywords into the search bar. For starters, look for jams on Newton's first law, second law, and third law, as well as gravity and inertia.

VIDEOS

Force and Motion

https://www.youtube.com/watch?v=xUCYFof8QyA

This video provides a great summary of the relationship between forces and motion.

Motion and Friction | Fun Science Lesson for Kids

https://www.youtube.com/watch?v=9ePpWrvOXGY

See a model of motion and friction in action in this engaging video.

Index

Page numbers in **boldface** refer to images.

About the Author

Kristin Thiel has written many titles for Cavendish Square Publishing, from books on science and technology, to biographies, to titles on history and current affairs. Her first was a biography of Dorothy Hodgkin, a Nobel Prize–winning crystallographer. She is the author of *Science Investigators: Investigating Light and Sound Through Modeling*.